Chedworth Roman Villa

Gloucestershire

Living in luxury

CHEDWORTH ROMAN VILLA lies in a little wooded combe in the Cotswold hills, looking down on to the beautiful green valley of the River Coln, which flows eventually into the Thames. A spring rises in one corner of the site, and was probably the main reason for settling on that spot. Excavation has revealed evidence of occupation from the Middle Iron Age, but the Roman-period remains are the most important. In the 4th century AD it was one of the grandest country houses in the whole of Roman Britain.

This house comprised over 50 rooms, including two bath-houses, dining rooms, heated living rooms, a water-shrine, a garden courtyard and even a lavatory with running water. The rooms were arranged in long wings on three sides of a rectangle about 120 × 90 metres, with a pillared portico running all round the inside edge. Above the portico rose a tall pitched roof covered with Cotswold limestone tiles.

The running figure symbolises Spring; from the dining room mosaic. The four seasons were a common motif on Roman mosaic floors

These sandalled feet are all that is left of a statue that once adorned the villa. It was probably of a household god

Underfloor central heating was one of the luxury features of the villa

Built to impress

The villa was a huge building, and anyone approaching from the valley bottom would have passed between the towering long wings to north and south, climbed the steep steps into the inner courtyard, and perhaps been admitted to the west wing, the 'inner sanctum' of the villa's owner. Once inside, the fine mosaic floors in every room, the vivid painted decoration on the plastered walls, and the comfort of heated floors underfoot would have completed the picture of grandeur, wealth and power which the house was built to convey.

Local traditions, shared culture

A feast in the dining room, a long, languid afternoon in the bath-house, spiritual refreshment in the shrine – all these activities represented the height of luxury in this far corner of the Roman world. Archaeologists generally agree that the big villas of the 4th century were the homes of powerful British families, who had grown rich under the Roman system of local self-government. The villa was built mainly in the 4th century, 300 years after the Roman invasion, by which time Britain had developed its own styles of building and design, adapted to the local climate and materials. Chedworth is very much a product of this native architecture, and not like a typical Roman country house as described by many Latin authors. But there are enough of the trappings of 'Roman' life – mosaics, wall-paintings, baths – to show that whoever lived here was very much a part of the wider empire, and shared in the culture of the social élite, which was enjoyed from northern Britain to north Africa, from Portugal to Syria.

It is these luxurious features that furnish us with our picture of the Roman Empire, and their survival in the Cotswold countryside is testimony to the incredible extent to which Roman culture permeated the ancient world.

Discovery

The villa was discovered in 1864 – according to legend by two local men out rabbiting in the woods. They had to dig for their ferret, which had gone to ground, and came across a section of mosaic pavement. One of the men is thought to have been Thomas Margetts, an under-gamekeeper on the Stowell Park estate. The other has recently been identified as Charles Higgins of Bibury by his great-granddaughter, Mrs Moon, although the story passed down in her family was that he had been out poaching.

An article in the *Gentleman's Magazine* relates how it took 'the superior intellect of the master' to recognise the handful of stones produced by the two men as *tesserae* from a Roman floor, but presumably they had realised that something special had been found. Once the find had been brought to the attention of the young Lord Eldon, heir to the Stowell Park estate, the investigation of the site was taken on by his uncle, James Farrer, who was a keen antiquarian.

Frederick 'Gramps' Norman

In 1930 the *Gloucestershire Echo* took Fred Norman back to the villa he had helped to excavate as a young boy. His reminiscences remain the only reminder of the local men who carried out the excavation.

Uncovering the ruins

In July 1864, up to 50 local men were put to work clearing the ruins. They felled the trees and shrubs, and removed the mass of soil burying the Roman house. Amongst them were Frederick Norman, Frederick Lawrence, Giles and William Coates and Thomas Margetts, who were farm labourers, gamekeepers and foresters. The chance to work on the villa must have been a rare excitement in the routine rural life of

The excavated bath-house as illustrated in the Journal of the British Archaeological Association in 1868

(Above) Chedworth Roman Villa could not have functioned without water. The spring at the north-west corner of the site fed the complex suites of bath-houses, kitchen and the latrine. This illustration appeared in an early report on the excavations published in 1868

the time – the railway had not yet reached Chedworth in 1864.

Under James Farrer's supervision, the majority of the Roman walls and floors were uncovered in the space of a few months. There are no surviving notebooks, drawings or photographs, and only one short publication of the findings. The artefacts from the dig form the basis of the museum collection as it is now, but we can only guess at what the enthusiastic amateur diggers missed. They certainly removed all later evidence from within the corridors and rooms, but luckily they left a great deal of archaeology intact. What is so special about Chedworth is that the owner decided to preserve the products of all that hard digging, and consolidate and protect the walls and major features which those local men had uncovered. The legacy of that busy summer of archaeological exploration is what you see here today.

What about Plumb?

A Northleach man called William Plumb had explored the humps and bumps in the woods in 1863. In a letter to a local historian, he revealed how he had found extensive walls and other evidence of Roman occupation on one of his rambles.

Discovery or rediscovery?

The villa ruins were certainly known in the 17th century, as a large lime-kiln was built on the bank above the north wing, dated by a Charles II penny. The Roman masonry would have made an ideal source of handy-sized limestone pieces for burning in the kiln. It is thought that the lime was used in the building of Cassey Compton house, about 2 km north of the villa.

Roman Britain

Britain was a province of the Roman Empire for over 350 years. Although not all the country was conquered, Roman remains have been found from Cornwall to Scotland, from Wales to East Anglia. Before the invasion of Emperor Claudius's legions in AD43, Britain was a land divided into many small tribal kingdoms, with a culture recognisable as part of the widespread Celtic people of Europe. But there is evidence of long contact with the Roman world before invasion, in the form of pottery, coins and other imported artefacts.

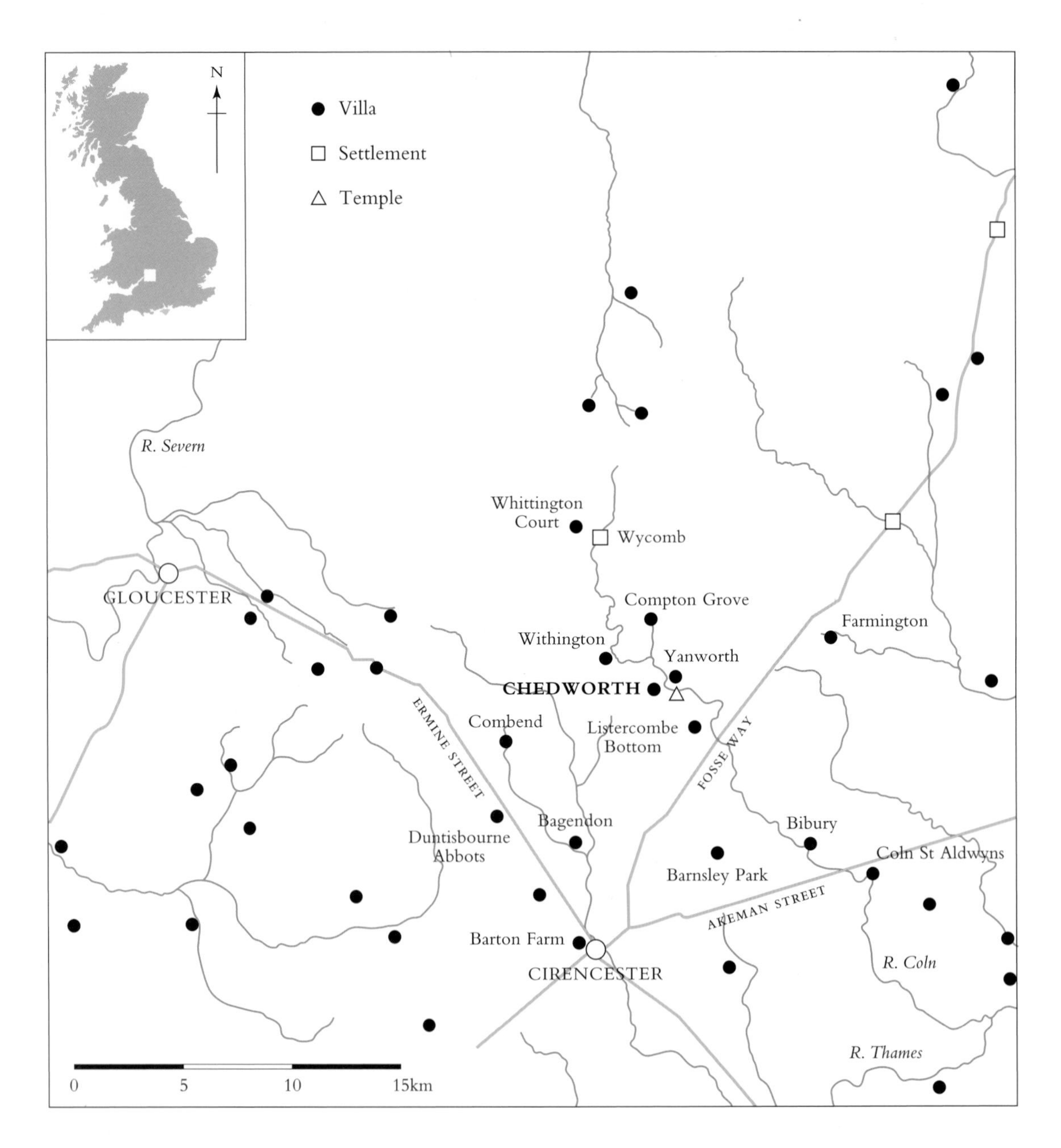

The Romans reach the Cotswolds

The Cotswolds was part of the kingdom of the Dobunni, who had their tribal centre at Bagendon near Cirencester. The Dobunni did not resist the Roman armies, and their territory was always prosperous and heavily 'Romanised' during the centuries of occupation. By AD 100 the towns of Glevum (Gloucester) and Corinium Dobunnorum (Cirencester) had been founded, and the first modest villas had been built. The network of roads and towns introduced by the Romans enabled military, political, and economic control of the country.

Under the *Pax Romana* the province became stable and wealthy, a source of grain, tin, hunting dogs, woollen goods and slaves for the Romans. The Roman system of government was a sort of franchise: local leaders were rewarded for co-operation with lands, contracts to supply the army, tax-collecting privileges and so on. The local civic leaders were essentially the native aristocracy, who were the most influenced by Roman culture.

Corinium rapidly became one of the richest towns of Roman Britain with grand public buildings, great religious monuments and richly furnished town houses. The countryside of the province developed more slowly, relatively small villas appearing only in the 2nd century. At Chedworth we think the earliest Roman-style rectangular stone house was built towards the end of the 2nd century.

The fruits of wealth

We can detect major changes in the 4th century from the archaeological evidence (written sources are very few). During this century a small number of very large and wealthy rural villas appeared, and investment in, and renewal of, town buildings apparently declined. All this suggests fundamental social and economic change.

It is still not clear why, but it seems that weakening of central government created a concentration of wealth in fewer hands. This enabled the construction of several massive palatial villas, of which Chedworth is one. At the same time, the administration of Britain was reorganised, and Corinium became the capital of one of the four newly created provinces of Britannia. So Chedworth was built anew in the hinterland of one of Britain's most important cities, with all the luxuries that money could buy.

Britannia abandoned

The end of Roman Britain has traditionally been put at AD 410, when the defence of Britannia was abandoned by the government in Rome. Archaeology tells us that some semblance of Romano-British life carried on well into the 5th century, but it is clear that the economy suffered major collapse around 410–20. The days of the great villas were certainly over, and as they fell into disrepair, parts continued to be used as storehouses and simpler dwellings.

(Left) Chedworth lies in an area that is rich in ancient sites, including many other Roman villas

(Right) This elaborately carved stone capital powerfully suggests the grandeur of Roman Corinium (modern Cirencester). It was unearthed in the town in 1838

What is a villa?

A *villa*, to the Roman world, was a farm. The key to wealth and social standing in the ancient world was ownership of land, and the classical vision of the Roman villa epitomised this ideal. The Roman gentleman should have a country house surrounded by farmland, where his slaves and servants worked to fill the house with the fruits of the earth. He should also participate in civic life and have a dwelling in the local town or city, which was regarded as the hub of social and political life.

A long, long way from Rome

The large British villas represent the greatest extent of Romanisation in the British countryside. Latin authors such as Pliny the Younger describe life in the wealthy villas of Italy, but without contemporary historical sources from Roman Britain, it is very difficult to tell how similar British houses were used. Archaeology can point out the differences as well as the similarities with continental models, and it seems clear that Roman Britain had its own characteristic indigenous version of the great house in the 4th century. For example, large British villas had more underfloor heating systems, and the rooms were more strictly arranged in long rows (wings) than in Italy. Similarities are obvious in the presence of mosaics, painted wall-plaster and pillared porticoes.

Grandest of the grand

There are approximately 1,000 known villa sites in Britain, ranging from small, plain houses with a few rooms to grand and complex sites with dozens of rooms, many mosaics and multiple courtyards. These villas were built throughout the Roman period, and the larger ones typically show evidence of occupation over several centuries. Approximately one per cent of villa sites fall into the category of very large, with several courtyards. Chedworth Roman Villa is one of these exceptionally large sites, interpreted (generally) as the homes of the wealthiest élite of Roman Britain. All of the known sites of this type reached their peak of extent and luxury of decoration in the 4th century.

Sustained by farming

Villa sites in Britain are clearly the centres of farms for the most part. Archaeology has revealed field systems and cattle pens, as well as granaries and barns. Tools, millstones, ploughshares,

(Right) Surviving fragments of painted plaster reveal that the villa was richly decorated inside

(Above) Chedworth Roman Villa lies in an area of very fertile farmland and woods

A 5th-century villa in Gaul very similar to Chedworth

'On the west rises a big hill, pretty steep but not rocky, from which issue two lower spurs, like branches from a double trunk, extending over an area of about four jugera. But while the ground opens out enough to form a broad approach to the front door, the straight slopes on either side lead a valley right to the boundary of the villa, which faces north and south. On the south-west are the baths, which so closely adjoin a wooded eminence that if timber is cut on the hill above, the piles of logs slide down almost by their own weight, and are brought up against the very mouth of the furnace.'

Sidonius Apollinaris, *Bishop of Clermont*

and even the evidence of charred grains, are all other indicators of farming practice. Sidonius described his Gaulish villa as having 'spreading woods and flowery meadows, pastures rich in cattle and a wealth of hardy shepherds.'

Is Chedworth really a villa?

Chedworth is slightly unusual in that it has not yet revealed traces of outer 'farmyard' courtyards as seen at other sites. This has led to other interpretations of Chedworth, most notably as a sort of pilgrims' hostel, a base for worship at various temples and shrines in the vicinity.

Who lived here?

Our contemporary written sources from Roman Britain are very few. Archaeological finds give us the physical remains of the people, from burials, as well as their personal possessions – rings, bracelets, bone hairpins, brooches. One such personalised item was found at Chedworth, a silver spoon of the mid-4th century inscribed with the name *Censorinus*. This is the only name we have from Chedworth. The only Roman burial found was that of an infant, two–three years old, interred in a stone-lined grave just outside the south wing.

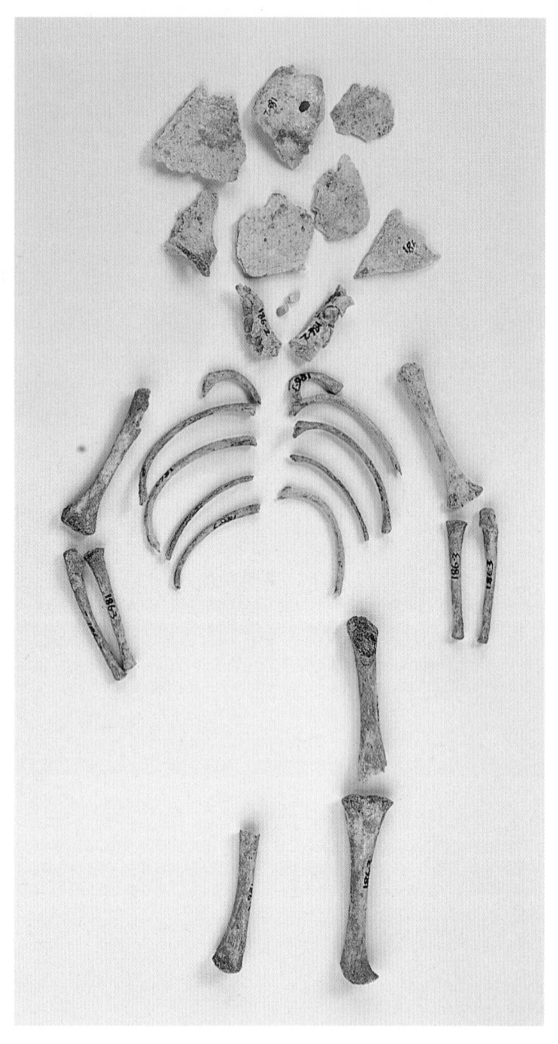

These bones of a young child are the only physical remains found of someone who lived at Chedworth in Roman times

A family of wealth and power

So what do we know about our Chedworth family? One certainty is that they were among the richest families in the whole of 4th-century Britain. With wealth went power, and we can infer that they were major players in the local government of the Dobunni. As Corinium was the capital of *Britannia Prima*, one of the four provinces of Roman Britain, the family may well have been involved in the control of a large area of Britain.

Britons become Romans

Archaeologists now believe that there were never very many genuine Roman Romans living in Britain: it has been estimated that out of a population of between 3.5 and 6 million, only 250,000 were Romans, mostly in the army. And the soldiers came from all over the empire.

(Left)
A copper alloy spoon excavated at Chedworth

(Right)
A reconstruction of the bath-house in the west wing

The vision of Romans arriving and building houses in the British countryside is outdated. On more and more villa sites, there is evidence of some continuity of occupation from the Iron Age, and we believe that most of these sites were occupied by native British families who had lived there for many generations.

After 300 years of Roman influence, a hybrid Romano-British culture evolved, and it is likely that the social élite of Britain (as in other parts of the Empire) regarded themselves as Roman. They certainly aspired to Roman-style trappings and luxuries, such as mosaic floors and painted walls. In contrast, the vast majority of Britons continued to live in traditional wooden round houses throughout the Roman period.

So we can speculate that Chedworth was the country seat of a wealthy and powerful family of the Dobunnic nobility, along with their servants and slaves. We do not know for certain, but a good guess might be that 100+ people lived at the villa, with its 50+ rooms, two bath-houses, and so on. It would have been a busy community in its own right, closely linked to the local city, and in easy communication with the rest of Britain via the 'motorway' of the Fosse Way.

People stories

We know nothing of Censorinus, apart from his name. Likewise, the child will remain for us just a skeleton, without name or even gender – it is not possible to tell the sex of very young children just from their skeletons. But these are tangible relics of the people who lived at Chedworth, and remind us that archaeology is about people and their stories.

How did the building work?

The Chedworth villa had a layout shared by many large rural houses in the north-western provinces of the Roman Empire. The rooms were set out in long rows or wings, connected to each other by a colonnaded corridor or portico, around a central open space. The Chedworth villa measured some 120m east–west, and about 90m north–south, and faced to the east. There was an inner courtyard reached by a flight of steps, and an outer court lower down to the east. At other large villas, a series of additional enclosures with agricultural buildings is usual, but these have not been found here.

Richly decorated inside and out

As well as the surviving walls, which give us the layout of the rooms, the evidence from Chedworth – portico pillars, stone roof tiles, window glass, and many fragments of carved decorative stones – enable us to picture the villa as it may have looked. The stone roof tiles tell us that the roof would have been steeply pitched. The height of the portico pillars suggests that the portico roof would have joined the main building well above head height, requiring windows above to get any natural light into the rooms. By looking at the evidence in a logical way, we can deduce that the building must have been a tall single-storey construction. The large collection of shaped architectural stone fragments tells us that the villa was very richly decorated on the outside.

Not all the rooms can be assigned a particular function, but it is clear that the luxury of mosaic floors and underfloor heating was spread throughout the house. Only those rooms used as kitchens and storerooms lack these features. The rooms in the west wing form a self-contained unit, and we can guess that these were the private apartments of the head of the household. The presence of more than one bath-house, kitchen and dining room, suggests that the house may have contained several households, presumably parts of the same extended family.

An impressive approach

What is clear is that the house was built to be approached from the east, by a trackway leading up from the River Coln. As a symbol of wealth and power, there could have been nothing more striking than the walk up through the lower court, with the bulk of the north and south wings towering on either side (the south wing may have been two-storey, to balance the height of the north wing up on its terrace). A climb up steep stone steps, through a gate-house, would have brought the visitor into the inner courtyard. There was still a 30m walk across to the west wing, the inner sanctum of the complex. We must imagine that here the head of our Chedworth family – perhaps Censorinus himself – held court. The villa was undoubtedly built as a display of social and political status, and the effect on visitors, even those from other, more developed, parts of the Empire, must have been very powerful.

(Left) The north wing. The villa was laid out as long rows of rooms linked by a corridor or portico

(Right) The portico that ran round the inner courtyard was paved with mosaic

Features of the villa

Chedworth has some remarkable surviving features, which illustrate the daily life of the inhabitants:

- Two bath-houses
- An octagonal cistern inside a shrine or temple – with the natural spring still running
- Fragments of twelve different mosaic floors *in situ*
- Several *hypocaust* underfloor heating systems, in various different styles
- Ceramic flue-tiles from the *hypocaust* systems still in place
- Over 30 rooms exposed (out of more than 50 originally)
- About 2km of standing walls
- Areas of painted wall-plaster still *in situ*
- The largest collection of shaped stone architectural fragments from any UK villa site
- A large collection of finds, including pottery, coins, bones, bone objects, iron tools, jewellery, glass, lead piping, building materials and carved stone

A wealthy family

All the material and other evidence that we have tell us a great deal about the people who lived at Chedworth and their way of life.

The sheer size of the villa is the first indicator of great wealth. There are only about ten sites known in Britain with so many rooms. Having two bath-houses is also very unusual, and the presence of an indoor lavatory with running water (Room 4) confirms the high status of the owning family. Having so many fine mosaic floors is another major demonstration of conspicuous wealth – apart from the still-surviving fragments of a dozen or so floors, the thousands of loose *tesserae* found indicate many more which have perished. Apart from the fixtures and fittings of the house, the presence of imported pottery, especially fragments of amphorae (vases) used to transport olive oil and wine, also implies wealth.

(Right) The dining room floor (Room 5) is the best preserved of the many mosaics at Chedworth

No gold?

No gold or silver objects are in the museum collection – the only known silver object from the site (Censorinus's spoon) has long since disappeared. However, this is not unusual. Gold and silver were rarely lost in antiquity, due to their very high value, and objects were often melted down and reused.

(Above) Several of the columns that once supported the portico have survived

(Right) The octagonal cistern has been filled by the same spring for 1600 years

Mosaics

(Above) The hooded figure of Winter; from the dining room mosaic (Room 5)

How did they do it?

There is still argument as to how the mosaics were created – were they built on the spot from individual stones, or made in sections in the workshop and brought to the site to be laid? One thing is certain – the many thousands of *tesserae* required for each floor had to be sawn, polished and chipped from the natural stone. This must have been done by a huge number of slaves and other workers, with the master-craftsmen creating the final complex designs.

All the Chedworth mosaics have a limited palette of four or five colours, all those of natural stones found locally, apart from the terracotta red, where ceramic tiles have been cut up and reused as *tesserae*.

The ultimate symbol of Roman culture, mosaic floors demonstrated the high status of their owners more than anything else. The floors at Chedworth all date from the 4th century, and are the products of a famous workshop based in Corinium. Many of the geometric motifs of the Chedworth mosaics can be seen in other floors in all parts of the Roman world. The running ribbon or guilloche around the borders is typical of the 4th century, and the acanthus scroll is also seen elsewhere.

The biggest mosaic at Chedworth is the dining-room floor in the west wing. The layout of the mosaic in two distinct areas – one with geometric patterns, one with figurative pictures – tells us it was a dining room. This was a typical Roman arrangement, with the diners seated at the patterned end, being able to admire the marvel of the mosaic pictures throughout their meal.

The illustrated area had suffered much during burial, but consists of eight polygonal panels arranged around a central picture (now lost). This central figure was almost certainly Bacchus, the god of wine and revelry, the surrounding scenes showing satyrs and maenads engaged in various 'party' activities!

(Right) Mosaic fragment of an urn

(Far right) Watercolour of part of the mosaic in the corridor of the west wing. This was uncovered in 2000 and reburied to protect it

Scenes from daily life

Bathing

One of the aspects of Roman culture which can be found in every corner of the Empire is the Roman bath. The Romans themselves inherited the idea of the heated bath from the Greeks, who used the *hypocaust* ('fire below') system to heat sweat-rooms and hot-water baths from the 5th century BC onwards. The practice spread and became one of the symbols of civilisation to the Romans, with the vast and elaborate public baths of Rome copied (usually on a smaller scale) in every town across all the conquered lands.

Chedworth villa had two bath-houses, which operated at the same time. The one in the north wing was a 'Spartan' bath, a *laconicum*, resembling a modern sauna. It had two small sweating-chambers, heated from furnaces outside the building, and a large cold plunge bath with two smaller ones adjacent. The largest room, the changing room, was probably used as a gym for exercises.

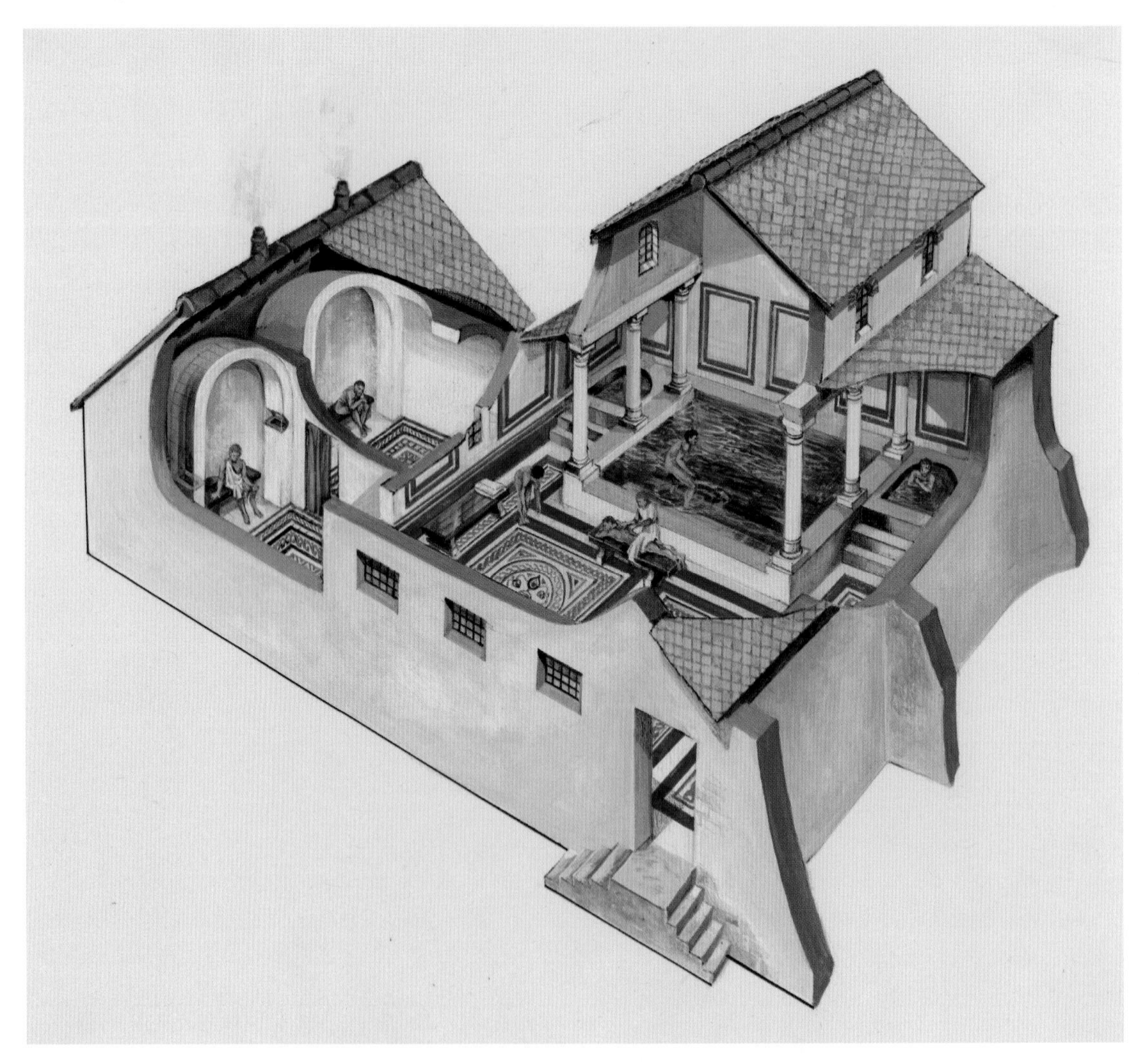

A reconstruction of the laconicum ('Spartan' bath-house) in the north wing (Rooms 21–23)

Flushed with success

The Chedworth villa also contained a rare example of a domestic latrine, with running water (Room 4). Shallow channels in the floor served to flush the latrine, and provide clean water for washing the sponges used for personal hygiene. The toilet seat would have been a long wooden bench, with holes cut in it – no separate cubicles, or division into ladies and gents.

The other bath-house in the west wing was more like a modern Turkish bath, with a steam room. This set of rooms has a classic Roman arrangement, with changing room (*apodyterium*), cool room (*frigidarium*) and intermediate and hot rooms (*tepidarium* and *caldarium*). There was also a cold plunge bath with painted decoration pretending to be marble (Rooms 10–16).

A communal activity

Bathing was clearly a leisure activity, and written records from Italy tell us it was a social one, with games and pastimes, chat and exercise, and maybe a massage, all in the company of friends, family or guests. Several game counters, and even a game-board roughly scratched on to a stone, have been found at Chedworth. Perhaps these were used to while away those long languid hours in the bath-house. The Roman bath involved covering the body with olive oil, and sitting in rooms at different temperatures to induce sweating. The oil, which soaked up the dirt from the skin, was then scraped off with a curved metal *strigil*. The bath was ended with a plunge into cold water, to close the pores and wake you up.

(Right) Bathers covered themselves in oil from the flask and then sweated out the dirt from their skin, which was scraped off with the curved strigil

Worship

The people of Roman Britain lived with the physical symbols of their religion all around them. The feet of two statues in the site museum are all that is left of the images of household gods, which were placed in niches around the house. There are several portable altars etched with rough depictions of personal gods. And the house had its own small temple or shrine, built over the cistern and its spring. The stone altar found here is missing the bronze statue which once stood on top, but we can be sure that it was the *genius* or guardian spirit of the spring, as water sources and other natural features were sacred to the Britons.

A hybrid religion

The religion of the country was a mixture of Roman and native Celtic elements, and often local gods and goddesses had the attributes of a

A reconstruction of the temple that was built over the spring at the north-west corner of the villa

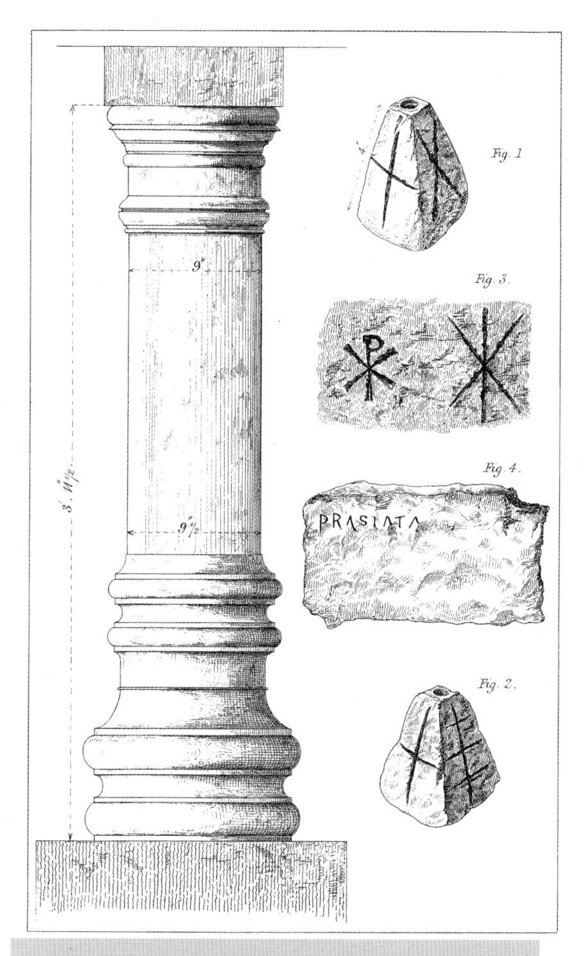

The temple by the river

About 1 km away, along the River Coln towards the Fosse Way, the remains of a very large Romano-British temple were excavated in 1865 and 1925. There is clearly a terraced platform, and some enormous stone blocks from the foundations remain. A pit in the centre of the temple revealed deer antlers, and some fragments of human bone. Some scholars have suggested this was one of the largest temples of Roman Britain. Control of such a temple and its revenues may have been a source of the Chedworth family's wealth.

Roman god added: a good example is *Sulis Minerva*, the patron goddess of the thermal springs at Bath. The Cotswold region had its own particular gods, most notably the Three Mothers (*Deae Matres*), and the peculiar little hooded trio, the *Genii Cucullati*. Recent scholarship has identified a healing goddess, *Cuda*, after whom the Cotswold area may be named. Her symbol was the pigeon – perhaps the bird depicted in the mosaic of the west bath-house changing room represents her.

Were the villa inhabitants ever Christians?

Several small Christian graffiti have been found scored into stones from the villa. They are all the simple chi-rho figure, the first two letters of Christ's name in Greek, and were found on stones that had once been set around the octagonal cistern in the water shrine. Some scholars have stated that this means the villa family were Christians; but the stones had been reused elsewhere, and the small size and random positions of the graffiti suggest that they were not prominently displayed when made. Perhaps a passing Christian made the unobtrusive marks as a sign to others sharing the faith?

(Right) The pigeon was the symbol of the local goddess Cuda. The mosaic in the west bath-house may represent it

Keeping warm

The *hypocaust* heating system was used not only in the baths, but also to warm the living rooms of the villa. These domestic central-heating systems are more common in the colder northern provinces than in the sunnier areas of the Roman Empire.

The system worked by passing hot air through a space under the floors, transferring heat from a fire lit outside the building, and venting the smoke at the eaves via flues hidden inside the walls. The floors were made of thick layers of stone and mortar, and acted very much like a modern storage heater. They were slow to warm up, but would retain their heat for a long time, so did not need a continuous fire.

Togas or trousers?

From what we know of written descriptions, wall-paintings and archaeological finds, the people of Roman Britain dressed appropriately for the climate – in trousers and tunics rather than togas. They also had a distinctive native national dress, the *Birrus Britannicus*. This was a short hooded coat, which the figure of Winter in the dining-room mosaic can be seen wearing. There are records of these clothes being exported from Britain – woollen cloth and garments may have been important trade goods.

At Chedworth there are examples of three different types of *hypocaust*:

The 'top-of-the-range' pillared type

Visible in Room 26 in the north wing. The floor was supported by shaped stone pillars, giving a continuous gap under the floor, and ensuring an even heat across the room.

The shallow-channelled type

Has just a few narrow channels carrying the hot air across the room. Examples of this also survive in the north wing (Room 24a).

The deep-channel and 'island' type

As seen in the dining room of the west wing (Room 5). This consisted of a number of geometrical stone 'islands', with channels up to 75cm deep and 40cm wide running between them. This would make use of the 'islands' as heat stores, and perform somewhere between the first two types.

Where did they sleep?

There are no rooms which can be identified archaeologically as bedrooms. In a single-storey house, it seems most likely that living rooms doubled as bedrooms at night – especially if the *hypocaust* was on in the winter.

All for show?

The presence of so many heated rooms begs several questions. How did they supply all the furnaces with wood or charcoal? Were all the *hypocausts* working at the same time? (This would have been very smoky.) How many slaves were on *hypocaust*-stoking duty?

Interestingly, there is little evidence of severe burning in any of the stoke-holes or *hypocaust* systems. Were they ever used? Or was the whole great house just for show? The people of Chedworth would also have used braziers inside the rooms for additional heat.

The flues were made of rectangular ceramic box tiles, several of which can still be seen *in situ* at Chedworth. They were set into the walls and hidden from view beneath layers of plaster. They are easy to recognise archaeologically, as the flue tiles were marked all over their outer surfaces with a toothed comb. This was not for decoration, but to provide a key for the plaster.

(Left) A reconstruction of the living room in the north wing. The room was heated by a hypocaust that circulated warm air under the floor (Room 32)

(Right) The forest of stone pillars you see today once supported a stone floor. This was à de luxe hypocaust (Room 26)

Eating

Many people are familiar with images of Roman feasts and revelry, gained either from written descriptions or wall-paintings of the period. It is tempting to assume that the classical arrangement of three couches around a low table was the pattern for the Empire as a whole. We find it hard to shake off visions of wealthy Romans reclining, while gorging themselves on exotic dishes. There is no evidence for this habit in Britain; indeed, some suggestions from archaeological fragments point more to the use of chairs and a higher table for dining.

Meal-time entertainment

We can, however, identify distinctly Roman traits in the layout of the dining room at Chedworth. Firstly, we can confidently say that Room 5 in the west wing is a dining room (Latin *triclinium* meaning 'three couches') from its division into two distinct parts. This is best seen in the mosaic floor: one end has plainer geometric patterns; the other has figurative pictures. Along the join between the two mosaic zones can be seen a small buttress sticking out from the main wall on either side, further marking the change. In Roman tradition, one area was used for eating the meal, the other for simply looking and marvelling at, or as a stage for entertainment. In Chedworth's case, the geometric end was where host and guests enjoyed their meals – and looked out over the splendour of the Bacchic scenes on the other part of the floor.

On the menu

Bone evidence from the site tells us they were eating beef, pork, mutton/lamb, venison and probably pheasant or other wildfowl. There are also many oyster shells. We have no physical remains of other foodstuffs from the 4th-century levels, but the pottery finds include cooking pots, *mortaria* (wide shallow bowls with grits fired into the inner surface for grinding herbs and seeds), strainers, cheese-presses and quern

(Above right)
A reconstruction of the dining room in use

(Left)
The kitchen

(Right)
A hare in the Winter mosaic. The villa's owners enjoyed a rich, varied diet

stones for grinding grain. It seems that the owners of Chedworth enjoyed a very varied diet, as befitted one of the richest families in the land.

The kitchens

There are traces of two kitchens, one at the junction of the west and south wings (Room 3), the other towards the east end of the north wing (Room 30). The south-west kitchen contained evidence of a large clay oven, and many fragments of cooking pots and storage jars. The presence of two kitchens may indicate that more than one household was living in the big house – perhaps the private household of the head of the family, and that of his sons or brothers.

The finds

(Right) This bronze ring is part of a horse harness

Fragment of decorated Samian Ware bowl. This fine tableware was imported from Gaul

Amphora handle. These large jars were used to transport bulk liquids such as olive oil and wine

Bone hairpins. They tell us that women wore their long hair pinned up

(Above left) *Stone altar, found in the water shrine. The holes in the top were for fixing a statue of the spring deity, probably of bronze (not found)*

(Above) *limestone relief depicting a hunter-god, with hound. A deer is shown on the right*

(Left) *Portable altar, with a crude relief of a deity*

(Right, above) *Rare pewter libation cup, used in religious rituals. It was recovered in 1998 from the north wing*

(Right, below) *Scales with lead weights, perhaps for weighing kitchen ingredients*

72.B

Villa people: 140 years of care and exploration

Many people have been involved with the Roman villa over the years, and all have contributed to the long process of caring for and understanding the villa. Here are some of their stories.

Discoverers

JAMES FARRER (1812–79)
Uncle of Lord Eldon, the landowner in 1864, Farrer directed the original excavations. His home was in Yorkshire, at Ingleborough Hall, and he also had estates in Scotland. Farrer was a well-known antiquarian, excavating Scottish brochs and ancient barrows, as well as the Chedworth villa. He was an MP and a lawyer by profession. James Farrer must be credited with planning and directing the original excavation. He also wrote the only account of the 1864 dig, but unfortunately left no notes, plans or photographs. Farrer also set in train the protection of the site, ordering the erection of the site shelters and the protective capping of the walls.

EARL OF ELDON (1845–1926)
John Scott, 3rd Earl of Eldon was the land-owner when the villa was discovered. When he came of age in 1866, he took over the work at the villa, and oversaw the completion of the museum and shooting lodge. It seems that he fell out with his uncle, as Farrer left Stowell, and had no more to do with the villa. During the late 19th century, Eldon used the villa for shooting parties, with the Roman ruins forming a lovely backdrop to the well-kept gardens. The site was always open to casual visitors, and the caretakers who lived in the shooting lodge made money selling lemonade and postcards. The 3rd Earl made one more significant contribution to preserving the villa, when he successfully fought in Parliament to have the planned line of the railway moved further west, thereby avoiding the villa remains.

FRED NORMAN (1849–1940)
Frederick Norman was a labourer living in Chedworth, and as a young man worked on the 1864 excavation. His account given to the *Echo* in 1930 is the only eye-witness description of

(Left)
The hypocaust photographed in the early 20th century by Henry Taunt

(Right, top)
The north-west corner of the site in the early 20th century. The best mosaics were roofed over to protect them

(Right, bottom)
The house in the centre of the site has been the home of the caretaker since it was built in 1868

the work which survives. On a Monday morning in June, at the age of fifteen, he accompanied other men from Chedworth to begin digging on the site:

About 3 o'clock Giles and Billy Coates had sunk a round hole like a post hole, and they came upon the pavement, and came and fetched we others. We started digging down to the pavement, and by night we had a piece of it uncovered ... On the next morning, everybody who came was put on the work, and there was about 50 of us digging, cutting the wood ... for the place was completely overgrown.

We went on and dug the best room out the very first start. The floor was all pavement when we uncovered it first, even where the patches of cement is now, but it perished as fast as we fetched out the earth. People later did come with their sticks and umbrellas and poke the pavement and they had to be stopped, but they loosened it and it had to be cemented. Thousands came while we were working on the villa. We were there about 3 years. There is nobody living who was there on the first day except me.

Fred Norman was the only one of the many local labouring men who excavated the villa to have his story recorded, so he has a special place in the site's history. Descendants of Mr Norman still visit the villa regularly.

(Above, left) Welbore St Clair Baddeley, who led the appeal for the money to acquire the site for the National Trust

(Above) Sir Ian Richmond, who carried out excavations at Chedworth in the 1950s and '60s

(Far right) Chedworth today

Investigators

WELBORE ST CLAIR BADDELEY (1856–1945)

St Clair Baddeley played a vital part in securing the future of the villa by helping to raise the money to buy the site for presentation to the National Trust. He was a poet, dramatist, traveller, archaeologist and historian from Painswick in Gloucestershire. He did some excavation work at the villa, and also dug at the temple site down by the river (originally looked at by Farrer in 1865). Through the offices of the Bristol and Glos. Archaeological Society, Baddeley led the campaign to raise £2,500 for the purchase of the Chedworth Villa site, when the Stowell Park estate came up for sale in 1924.

SIR IAN RICHMOND (1902–65)

The doyen of Roman-period experts, Richmond was a professor at Oxford University when he became archaeological adviser to the National Trust. In the late 1950s and early '60s Richmond spent a week or two every summer excavating at Chedworth, digging many small

Famous visitors

FRANCIS and HORACE DARWIN, sons of the great evolutionary theorist, visited the villa site in 1877 to collect information for Charles Darwin's research on the activities of earthworms and their role in burying ruins.

HER MAJESTY QUEEN ELIZABETH was reported to have visited the site incognito in the 1960s, accompanied by a lady-in-waiting. The Queen was attending the Cheltenham National Hunt festival.
Her grandson, PRINCE HARRY, visited the site on a school trip in the 1990s.

trenches in an effort to understand the archaeological sequence. He oversaw investigations in advance of wall repairs, and had a new shelter constructed over the north bath-house. He was never an aloof 'ivory tower' academic, always involving local workmen in the archaeology and feeding his discoveries back into publications, including a new guidebook. Sadly, he died suddenly in 1965, but his work represents the first serious investigations of the villa using modern scientific methods.

Curators

NORMAN IRVINE (1912–2001)

Norman Irvine came to live at the Roman villa with his family in 1918, his father being involved in forestry management. He went to school in Yanworth and Chedworth, leaving in 1926 to start work in the Stowell Park woods. The National Trust 'inherited' the Irvine family when it acquired the villa in 1924, Norman's mother being the first custodian. In 1930 Norman was appointed caretaker at the villa, and, with some job-title changes, stayed there for the next 47 years.

He was a great accumulator of information, and, although he left school at fourteen, Norman studied all the written sources about the villa, and wrote reams of careful notes about the site, which would put many scholars to shame. He worked with St Clair Baddeley and Prof. Richmond and learned a great deal about the archaeology of the villa. Having grown up there, he knew the locality intimately and was familiar with all the sites around.

Apart from the war years, Norman kept the grounds of the villa looking neat: 'you had to get up at 5 in the morning to mow the grass, if you wanted it to look good for the visitors' sums up Norman's dedication to his job. He and his wife Dorothy left the villa in 1977, just before the reception building was put up, but having seen the visitor figures grow from hundreds to the incredible peak of 78,000. And all of those were sold tickets from a window at the side of the house.

Seen by millions

Since visitor records were kept by the National Trust, well over three million visits have been made to Chedworth Roman Villa. It remains one of the most popular Roman sites in the UK.

The natural history of the villa

(Left)
A Pipistrelle bat

(Below)
A Long-eared bat

The villa today is a small haven for wildlife between the woods and the cultivated fields. It provides a variety of habitats, with open sunny banks, the cover buildings, and of course the walls of the Roman house. It is worth taking time when visiting the villa to look around at the rich fauna and flora. You might see masonry bees cutting pieces of leaf to make their nest chambers in the walls; or a vibrantly coloured pheasant descended from those brought to Britain by the Romans.

Bat food

The discarded wings of the larger, plumper moths are often found on the mosaic surfaces – the bats' favourite way of eating is to tear the wings from their prey and eat the bodies. Sometimes the tables are turned – the author has witnessed an owl swooping from the woodland edge to seize a bat in flight.

Bats

The rarest creatures which live at the villa are bats – it is one of the most important bat sites in the county. Pipistrelles and Long-eared bats live in the reception building and the Victorian house. Other species seen at the site include Lesser Horseshoe, Whiskered, Noctule and even the very rare Barbastelle. The flowery banks, with over 50 different species of wild flower recorded, support an abundant range of moths, which form the main diet of the nocturnal, insectivorous bats.

A Roman snail

Snails

The most distinctive creature to be seen about the villa is the large Roman snail (*Helix pomatia*). This species was introduced by the Romans as an edible delicacy. Snails are very fussy about habitat – presumably they came originally from the limestone foothills of the Alps in northern Italy. They thrive around the villa, hibernating in the crevices of the ancient walls.

Roman plants

The Romans introduced many new and improved food and medicinal plants to Britain. New cultivated varieties of plum and peach, many herbs such as oregano and marjoram, and even the stinging nettle, are amongst the introduced plants.

Trees

There are a number of non-native trees around the site, planted in the late 19th–early 20th centuries. Transplants from America were popular, including some very tall Western Red Cedars and two Buckeyes grafted on to native Horse Chestnut boles. The trees reflect the time the villa spent as a romantic ruin set in a beautifully tended garden landscape.

Unwelcome visitors

Some flora and fauna are not so welcome at the villa. The archaeological habits of the rabbits are fairly easy to deal with, but the danger to the ancient fabric comes from microscopic algae and lichens. These love to grow on the damp surfaces of ancient walls and floors inside the cover buildings. As the Roman masonry is attached to the ground, the movement of moisture up through the fabric can never be prevented. These kinds of growths can only be removed by skilled conservators.

Animal archaeologists

Larger animals such as fallow, roe and even muntjac deer can be seen in the woods, along with badger, fox, weasel, hare and of course the rabbit. Rabbits played a part in the discovery of the villa, and still like to dig for mosaics today.

Conservation in action

The villa has a long history of conservation. Indeed, it was one of the earliest sites in Britain to benefit from a deliberate philosophy of preservation and presentation to the public. The Victorian excavators moved rapidly to erect three wooden shelters over the best-surviving Roman remains, and to ensure that other vulnerable features were reburied. They also put protective cappings on the walls to preserve them, and of course built the museum to store and display the finds, along with the house in which a caretaker/curator has lived ever since.

Caring for Chedworth

Not all of this activity would be acceptable conservation practice today: for example, no records of all the changes and rebuilding works were kept. A great deal of the architectural subtlety of the Roman house has been lost, as collapsed walls were rebuilt and levelled off. But iron stoves were lit in the shelter buildings to prevent frost damage, and other features were covered with straw in the winters. Without the care and attention given to the site by its original

(Above)
The exposed remains of the hypercaust were protected from winter frosts with straw

(Left)
The shelter buildings still play a vital role in protecting the exposed mosaics

Radio-controlled conservation

There has been a long programme of environmental monitoring at the site, measuring variables such as temperature, relative humidity, moisture content, rainfall and so on. This has enabled us to understand how the Victorian shelters perform as conservation tools, and to suggest where they can be improved – or what kind of building would be needed to replace them. The sensors used for this monitoring send their readings by radio signal to a computer logger. This means a lot of data can be collected automatically, without laying wires all over the site.

explorers, there would be nothing left to see today.

Over the years, various interventions have been made into the mosaics, with one floor (the west bath-house changing room) having been lifted and relaid on an impermeable membrane. Small areas of other pavements have been repaired and relaid, but the majority of the mosaic astonishingly remains *in situ*, the *tesserae* still sitting where they were so carefully set nearly 2,000 years ago.

Observing change

Our approach to conservation today is somewhat different, as we try to preserve the surviving remains *in situ*. Efforts in recent years have concentrated on gaining a far more detailed understanding of the site. Conservation can proceed only through careful observation of change, so the villa has needed thorough surveying to produce a base record on which all observations and interventions can be recorded.

A balanced approach

The dangers to the Roman fabric are mainly from freeze/thaw cycles, salts deposited on surfaces as moisture evaporates, and biological growth. A good conservation solution would be to rebury the site, but as the National Trust is committed by statute to providing access to the historic sites it owns, this is not an option. Our conservation activity must concentrate on stabilising the surviving Roman fabric, while enabling visitors to see and enjoy it.

Spring cleaning

The mosaics are now cleaned annually. This is done with sponges, using de-ionised water (so no more salts are introduced). The cleaners must rest on padded boards so that their weight is spread. In the past, caretakers walked across the mosaics' surfaces, and swept with ordinary brooms. There is even a record of diesel fuel being used to give the mosaics a lovely shine! Not only salts and algae need to be cleaned off, but bat and bird droppings are also deposited on some floors.

(Right) Cleaning the mosaics in the 1970s

Recent archaeological work

Investigation has continued piecemeal since the 1960s, but during the last ten years systematic intervention has greatly increased our knowledge of the villa. This has included the following activities:

Geophysical surveys

Magnetometry and resistivity measurements have shown that the villa complex extends at least 20m beyond the National Trust boundary to the east. A clear trace of a double-ditched road or trackway has also been found, showing that the approach in Roman times was roughly from the modern river crossing, up the middle of the field to the east. The villa was clearly built to be at its most imposing and magnificent from this direction.

Garden court excavations

Three trenches in the inner courtyard searched for evidence of a formal garden, in the style described by many Latin authors, and as seen in surviving Roman wall-paintings. No trace of bedding trenches, pathways, raised beds, fountains or any other aspect of a classical garden was found. It seems that the tradition in Britain was different, and the Chedworth villa did not have a formal garden. In fact, the evidence suggested that the inner courtyard was grassed over as it is today. These excavations showed that the earliest evidence of the Roman period is concentrated at the west end of the site – that what became the west wing was the limit of the earliest villa, built during the 2nd century.

(Above and far right) Excavation in 2000 uncovered substantial areas of mosaic floor in the west wing

South wing excavations

Here a mirror-image of the north wing was found, with a corridor and room with *hypocaust*, showing that the luxury apartments of the house stretched all along the south wing. Even the corridor had its own shallow-channelled *hypocaust* heating system. For the first time, evidence of activity after the Roman period was recovered, charred grains and other debris suggesting the corridor was still in use in the 5th century, for storing or processing agricultural produce.

Lower garden excavation

In a deeper trench below modern vegetable gardens, a metalled trackway was uncovered from the later period of the house. Below, an earlier track and post-holes suggested this area was given over to farmyard activity when the villa was a more modest building. Further below, the amazing chance find of an infant burial took the site back to the Iron Age – Carbon-14 dates put the skeleton at 360 BC. We can infer that there was a settlement here then, as infants were buried close to dwellings at that time.

Buried mosaic survey

A series of small excavations was carried out in every room of the villa, to find any surviving traces of mosaic which had not been recorded in the past. Several mosaics were revealed and photographed in the west wing – including samples of the pavement which we now know runs the whole length of the west-wing corridor. A portion of the most recent mosaic (about AD 380) in the north wing (Room 28) was uncovered and showed that money was still being spent on the villa right up to the end of the Roman period.

This survey also helped to confirm that the villa did not slowly evolve as previously thought, but underwent a most dramatic expansion in the 4th century, with huge quantities of earth being moved about, and the bulk of the north and south wings being newly built. The west wing was completely remodelled, and most evidence of the earlier phases (2nd and 3rd centuries) was obliterated.

A thousand years of occupation

In summary, our recent work has dramatically improved our knowledge of the site. We know that Chedworth was occupied from at least the Middle Iron Age up to the advent of the Saxons into England – a period of nearly a thousand years. The grand 4th-century house can be put in some perspective as the time of its greatest flourishing, but it is not the whole story. The archaeology suggests a theme of continuity through history – perhaps descendants of the Iron Age family who buried their child outside their roundhouse in 360 BC were still bringing in the barley harvest and storing it in the ruined villa, long after the glory days of the Roman period had come and gone. Who knows, perhaps the local men who excavated the villa in Victorian times were uncovering the traces of their own direct forefathers.

The future

Chedworth not only needs conserving, but the access to the monument and interpretation of it also deserve to be improved – the Victorian shelters do not enable visitors to see the mosaics very well. The 9,000+ school visitors every year need a proper education room, and many other visitors cry out for a cup of tea.

New buildings

Our plans centre around a new facilities building, with education centre, storage for archaeological finds and archives, offices and workspace for volunteers; and a new cover building, better to protect and present the best of the Roman features which survive. This would also enable us to uncover and present the mosaics which are still buried, and finally show the whole suite of fine 4th-century floors in the west wing.

This will still take several years of planning and fundraising, and of course much discussion with our neighbours and other local communities.

In the meantime, we will continue to do our best to interpret and present the villa – there has been a programme of 'living history' events, and costumed interpretation for schools, for several years, which will continue. Chedworth remains the most-visited late Roman villa site in the UK.

Preserving antiquity and ambience

The National Trust is determined to make sure that any developments benefit the site. We must do our best to try to preserve not only the rare and incredible *in situ* remains from the height of the Roman period, but also the wonderful ambience that the 19th-century presentation created. The beauty and tranquillity of the site are prized by visitors. And we must also be grateful to the owners of the Stowell Park estate, who maintain the villa's picturesque setting.